DEADLIFTS

DEADLIFTS

✽

PATRICIA CLARK

NEW MICHIGAN PRESS
TUCSON, ARIZONA

NEW MICHIGAN PRESS
DEPT OF ENGLISH, P. O. BOX 210067
UNIVERSITY OF ARIZONA
TUCSON, AZ 85721-0067

<http://newmichiganpress.com>

Orders and queries to <nmp@thediagram.com>.

Copyright © 2018 by Patricia Clark.
All rights reserved.

ISBN 978-1-934832-63-9. FIRST PRINTING.

Printed in the United States of America.

Design by Ander Monson.

Cover art: Mary McDonnell, *Voices 6*:
marymcdonnellart.com

CONTENTS

Deadlifts   1
Alpha   2
In Memoriam Patricia Lou   3
The Memorial Service   4
Greek Obituary: A Trisagion Service   5
Middle Names   6
PJC of Canton, Ohio   7
Saying Farewell to the Powder Puff Beauty Salon   8
Riddle   9
Assemblage of a Life   10
Wounded   12
No Reason to be Sad Over Her Death   14
Kicking it Up   15
To Mexico   16
For You, A Love Poem   17
Romance Writer   18
Judge   19
On Not Speaking Ill of the Dead   20
What I Wanted   22
Our Lady of Victory Church   23

Acknowledgments   29

to Stan Krohmer, always

Some say, first, get rid of the body. Not me.
I say let the corpse dance. Make the living lie still.

—Richard Hugo

DEADLIFTS

They are dying all over America,
Patricia Clarks, one after another—

in Vine Grove, Kentucky, but also this town
of Grand Rapids, Michigan. How rude

for a friend to say, "I saw your
name in the obituaries. A shock

for a moment, thinking you gone."
Then we resumed working out,

picking up handles of bright
stretchy bands, the long iron

body bars, and then heavy
weights to do deadlifts.

ALPHA

The one who started it all, Patricia May
Clark (Corfixsen), who passed on July 18, 2016.

Though we lived together in the same town,
drove the Michigan Street hill when icy,

we never met. Your life written up in a few lines
and none of the agonies or raptures comes across.

To be a good Christian woman, that's a gift.
A member of Holy Spirit Church—I refused

to go there. A solid twenty-three years of time
separate your life, and mine. How different

we were! You took your husband's name, oh
good woman. I wouldn't give up mine,

or my identity. I see that one of your sisters
became a nun. In short, there's nothing we share

but a name, a walk on this earth in one
town. I lay a penny on each of your eyes.

IN MEMORIAM PATRICIA LOU

Sometimes their names have a musical note,
sometimes I am certain that our paths crossed.

And so, Patricia Lou, your name on the wind,
syllables carrying me back where we both began.

How often people ask, "Where were you born?"
The word tolls like a bell, steeple ring, bell on a rope,

mortality song, and there was Tacoma, Mount
Rainier, pulp mills, steelhead, skies reflecting gray,

rivers lined with Douglas fir, cottonwoods, birch.
Some places known best from the wrong end

of a telescope—gone, like born, that difficult tune.
In the year I started college, you married, and chose

to be born again. We were already diverging, you
and I, bells can be rung, variations, in so many ways.

I swore I'd never return to Tacoma. That part
wasn't true—I go back to the graves. And you?

THE MEMORIAL SERVICE

has ended—in fact,
it concluded in Tuscaloosa, Alabama

on Thursday, October 15, 2015.
What's left is a photo of the deceased,

a list of who remains, and traits
of this Patricia Clark that someone wrote

about her life—where she worked, what
it meant, nothing about why.

An itch to travel. A giggle. The beauty
of the face one presents to the world.

She would not be back to pack a bag
or grab a boarding pass. Her flights

over now. Two sons, one in Japan with wife,
two grandchildren. Magnolias, lilacs, a rose.

A list of pallbearers, all male. Donations to
the cloudy pewter sky or—amazing—call

and offer your services. My name again, writ
into a text block. And saved.

GREEK OBITUARY: A TRISAGION SERVICE

For some Patricia Clarks, few words:
no birthdate, no photo, no middle name.

On Dale Street, in Anaheim, California, a quick
mysterious goodbye. Why so little known?

The names of two cousins, Alex and Tom Soles.
O soul of the beloved niece of Georgia Soles.

A blade of grass, a leaf that drifted down.
Greek rituals followed to soothe their pain.

It was Thanksgiving and they tried to give
thanks. No photo could be found of her face.

MIDDLE NAMES

Patricia Ann of Yorba Linda, California must
stand distinct from Patricia Ann "Pat"

of Anna, Illinois. A democracy of names,
a ceremony of baptisms with hands dipped

in holy water, touched on foreheads, both cheeks
along with words said in front of community, priest,

God—"*This is who you are.*" Somehow I had a hole
for a middle name, an ache, a weltering wound,

and place that needed healing or filling up.
Came Confirmation time I knew my name—

I chose the one from Assisi, bearded holy man
who gave away his clothes and shoes, spent time

speaking to animals. I still want to go by train to East
Umbria, bowing my head in his birthplace,

as who can be contained by a nameless gray town
on Puget Sound, who can sense all that a name implies?

PJC OF CANTON, OHIO

They whirl together in the rainy trees,
Patricia Jean, cedar waxwings in a flock—

how beautiful it is that each obit lists a flock
of family. Everyone must be counted,

even your two brothers who sound like twins,
gone perhaps nearly as long as your parents.

Something in your gap-toothed smile tells me
what you added, working at Rite Aid Drugstore

twenty-two years. I want you back, want to lift
you from a car accident, carry you away instead

to your garden. Not to hoe, or weed, but to watch
your husband prune and trim. Sit here, rest.

SAYING FAREWELL TO THE POWDER PUFF BEAUTY SALON

Three husbands went to their graves before
Patricia Ann of Covington—she had a knack

for longevity, now giving up, loosening her grasp
at eighty-three. How many haircuts, perms,

shampoos and sets in fifty-two years in charge
of the Powder Puff Beauty Salon? Not only

that, but include another twenty-five of hair
done at the Covington Care Center. Her arms

and fingers could do hair in the dark, put
rollers in or blow hair into shape with a snap

of the switch. Organist for thirty-five, member
for over fifty years at church. And what's

this Apple Dumpling Gang she co-created?
Her list of survivors makes a sweet

litany of Ricky, Tricia, Tiffany and Josh—
Everett, Aspen, Connor, Caleb, more. Bless all!

RIDDLE

Who died on the eleventh of this month, the new year?
Who straggled up in Seattle, eight years after me?

Who drove to Oregon with her family, past Mt. Rainier, Mt
Hood, 1963, watershed year when all the poets died?

Would she know names Frost, Williams, Roethke, Plath?
Why, if she was ninth of ten children, are thirteen names

of siblings listed? Why am I caught again, her smiling face
gazing at me, saying—"Don't let me go, go!"

Why, in the snow today, ticking down like time-
bomb fragments, do I feel her breath warm on my neck?

ASSEMBLAGE OF A LIFE

We are all the same, these lives
bracketed by dates,

these lists—who preceded us, who
remains. Childhood in the Bronx,
one sister, two brothers.

First grade photo with a pleated skirt,
and outside with a new puppy.
Easter egg hunt in a pink
sweater.
Family around a Christmas tree
with silver strands,
star on the top.

Forgive me if I imagine wrong.

*Story within a story—second husband the love
of your life, Lawrence.*

Your jobs and work, travel
around the world.

Silver hair in a flattering bob,
dark skin.

You were known, always, as Pat.
I hear someone call your name
and turn.

WOUNDED

That the one whose face came up
was like me. For once,
no husband—the Clark name
hers alone.

No list of children that she named.

Instead, a first in all these notices
of death—a mention of music
she loved, especially the Beatles.

And how glad she was, Patty Ann
now flown, to have shared her birth-
day with Aretha Franklin,
Elton John.

That I couldn't let her story go—
why cooped up forty-two years?

That New England, upstate
New York, has hardwood forests,
dark shadows between trees,
snow that settles in, both
freezing mounds and insulation,
warmth in a heap.

That I found two more photos—
one with Patty and her two small
sisters—they all wore dresses
that matched.

In the last photo, 1964, Patty's on the left,
almost not in the picture, but her hand
stretches out, to shake Dick
Clark's hand after a concert.

Shadows between trees, bad cells
gone wrong to wreck a life.
*Once you knew her, you had a friend
to keep.*

Her favorite towns—Troy
and Waverly. Saint James Cemetery,
the final place.

NO REASON TO BE SAD OVER HER DEATH

So few lines sometimes, the story incomplete,
barely a sketch, a photo, some names, two dates—

fourteen lines in the case of poor Patricia Ann
of Paterson, New Jersey. Those are pearls

around her neck, and she's leaning into the photo as if
to say, "I'm here and still alive." One of her two sons

penned the words, proud to say she ran the court
playing tennis all through school, East Side

High, 1985. She was a loving mom, no note
on a husband and no explanation why she spent

"a brief time" in North Carolina. The slippery
self goes wriggling away without a chance

to be caught. Dead at the young age of forty-eight?
I'll bet anything she would have liked to stay.

KICKING IT UP

Somehow Patricia got turned into a name
of country western tunes, cowboy hats and boots—

Ricky Clark of Fredericksburg and, for once,
no date of your beginning to mark your age.

Your dance partner, though, of fifty-seven years
lives on, good ol' Thaddeus, aka Ted.

I like how this story goes—not a word
about parents, siblings, death. Ricky was

"cherished and admired." Five children live on
whispering that. I see them on the dance floor,

Ricky and Ted—what a circle they cut,
flourishes, dips, twirls, and tip of the hat.

TO MEXICO

    [with a line borrowed from Thomas Lux]

I begin again, sister, and it's true,
the devil's in my neck, but between you

and me, there must be more to connect us
than just a name. Patricia Rae Clark,

I like the tilt of your head, the lyrical list
of things you loved and a place, too,

Zihuatanejo, Mexico, where you settled a spot
for thirteen years, finding some warmth.

On my neck's this bowling ball of a complex head,
trying to make sense. How to live a life,

then how to exit with some grace. If my neck's
sore, it's the weight, heavy thought. Somehow

you just departed, saying goodbye with kisses, a touch.
Each obit's just a sketch—the mystery's all you.

FOR YOU, A LOVE POEM

Girls named after singers, or movie stars—
"All the rage, it's Patti Page," the blond crooner gone

in 2013. You, though, Patty Paige Clark, maybe no one
thought of her, naming you. A nursery rhyme,

the pat-a-cake one, invented just for us—
"Roll it, pat it, and sign it with a P—"

I suspect you were curly and blond as a child,
so how many of us does that make across the land?

One day it struck me the way the talon of a hawk
hits a mouse: researching today, there could be more.

The family requests no flowers though Patti's life
will be celebrated. Come, bring a story, your name.

ROMANCE WRITER

Out of rural Kent and a Sussex town called Hove,
out of a maternal line of writers going back

and back, out of a father working on the Baltic Exchange,
a corn broker selling futures, trading in corn.

I keep looking them up—never sure who's next,
how close to home they live, or how far away.

By the age of twelve she published her first
work, novellas for children. And where was I,

at twelve? Still roaming the hill with the twins,
catching polliwogs at the swamp, letting a brindle dog

lick my face. How do we grow into a self,
or a name? She wore Robins before Clark,

then morphed into Claire Lorrimer. I glimpse
an English house, lace waves at the window, a tea set

with cups. Someone is pouring tea, a table laid
for two. I lift a biscuit up, savoring the lemony bite.

Then there's a swoon, a gallant fellow, a punt
on the Thames, an engagement. Then, a death.

JUDGE

Where the journey starts, where it goes winding to an end,
Greenville, South Carolina and clear across the land

to Seattle, the watery coast, this can be traced.
Your parents gone, eldest of seven, you grieved

the loss of three siblings—Juanita, Phillip, John—
and moved away. It's not my place to invent who

you were. The photo shows you in a judge's robe.
Among all of us, you're the regal one.

There you preside in a courtroom, mind and voice at work.
It rings in my ears, your last gavel banging down.

ON NOT SPEAKING ILL OF THE DEAD

When you've never heard of Ponchatoula, Louisiana,
can't find it on a map, want to repeat its sounds,

when your mouth says some syllables are more sweet
than others—say bayou, jambalaya, magnolia,

when your mind can't imagine growing up there without
erasing the self, losing beaches of Washington State,

when you know the humid warmth of the gulf
frizzes hair and moistens layers of your skin,

when you must share a name with other girls,
another Patricia—with sisters like yours, four,

when she might look defiant, stubborn, mean,
in the only photo they could find—

(chin jutted out, thick jowls, eyes bright like
burning coals, nostrils flared)

when she threw up a hand, often, and said,
"Don't take my photo when I look like this—"

when they had to lay her down, mourning, in tears,
with no one writing a good line about her,

when you think what is fate, who is known before
the end, Bedico Cemetery her final spot.

WHAT I WANTED

I wanted to lift you up, especially you, Patricia M.,
from a state next to mine—for your dog Logan Blue,

who gets an obituary note, and for your high school
prom date, Jim Vash, whom you must have loved

but who doesn't seem to be the father of your four
kids. I wanted to celebrate with confetti and to know,

to pronounce my name, over and over, with death
in the back of my throat, to imagine the forthcoming lines

written for me, perhaps, woven with a dog's name
or two, leavened with a humorous note, a poem,

cinched by the belt of numerous towns I lived in, men
and others who I loved. Can the list go on?

I wanted to name books that bowled me over, birds I saw
or held, countries I flew to, oceans and deep lakes

waded in or swum across, slopes I skied at midnight,
food I couldn't live without. O earth, O trees.

OUR LADY OF VICTORY CHURCH

Out of a gingko leaf, a scrap of river birch bark,
out of a morning that sparkles, icicle drip and sun,

out of details that call to you the way peepers
will start chorusing in Lamberton Creek, soon,

"we're here, we're alive," so the few obit
paragraphs tell so many lives, ones worth

knowing—except it's too late. And isn't it time
for you, too, to reflect? Mrs. Clark of Hyannis Port,

no maiden name, no mention of where you began.
Living near the water, you recently persuaded friends

to donate sails to be recycled for sustenance fishermen
in Haiti. Only sixty years old at time of your death.

Wherever we end, the date, or time, let's listen up
and get to work! Sail on, bright boats through

Caribbean waters—pull in a fish, unhooking the lure
from a red snapper's lip—and let smoke rise from coals,

later, enjoying the flavors of a glorious final feast.
You're the one to whom we'll lift a glass.

ACKNOWLEDGMENTS

Many thanks to the editors of the following journals who published and encouraged my work:

"Deadlifts," *Adirondack Review*
"What I Wanted" & "Our Lady of Victory Church,"
 Prairie Schooner

Thanks to readers at New Michigan Press for going through a pile of manuscripts, and to Ander Monson, of course. Thanks, also, to the Mon/Wed strength training folks (you know who you are) at GVSU for laughs and good cheer, especially Terri Bacon-Baguley, who spied the first obit. And an especially warm thank you to Michigan native now NY artist Mary McDonnell for the use of her drawing for the cover.

PATRICIA CLARK is the author of five volumes of poetry, including most recently *The Canopy* (2017) and *Sunday Rising* (2013). She has also published two chapbooks: *Wreath for the Red Admiral* and *Given the Trees*. Her work has been featured on *Poetry Daily* and *Verse Daily*, and has appeared in *The Atlantic, Gettysburg Review, Poetry, Slate,* and *Stand*. She was a scholar at the Bread Loaf Writers Conference and has completed residencies at The MacDowell Colony, the Virginia Center for the Creative Arts, the Tyrone Guthrie Center (in County Monaghan (Ireland), and the Ragdale Colony. Awards for her work include a Creative Artist Grant in Michigan, the Mississippi Review Prize, the Gwendolyn Brooks Prize, and co-winner of the Lucille Medwick Prize from the Poetry Society of America. From 2005-2007 she was honored to serve as the poet laureate of Grand Rapids, Michigan. She is Poet-in-Residence and Professor in the Department of Writing at Grand Valley State University in Michigan.

❦

COLOPHON

Text is set in a digital version of Jenson, designed by Robert Slimbach in 1996, and based on the work of punchcutter, printer, and publisher Nicolas Jenson. The titles here are in Futura.

❁

NEW MICHIGAN PRESS, based in Tucson, Arizona, prints poetry and prose chapbooks, especially work that transcends traditional genre. Together with DIAGRAM, NMP sponsors a yearly chapbook competition.

DIAGRAM, a journal of text, art, and schematic, is published bimonthly at THEDIAGRAM.COM. Periodic print anthologies are available from the New Michigan Press at NEWMICHIGANPRESS.COM.

www.ingramcontent.com/pod-product-compliance
Lightning Source LLC
Chambersburg PA
CBHW031506040426
42444CB00007B/1233